# Who Works Here?

# Supermarket

by Lola M. Schaefer

Heinemann Library
Chicago, Illinois

© 2000 Reed Educational & Professional Publishing
Published by Heinemann Library,
an imprint of Reed Educational & Professional Publishing,
100 N. LaSalle, Suite 1010
Chicago, IL 60602
Customer Service 888-454-2279

Printed in Hong Kong
Designed by Made in Chicago Design Associates

04 03 02 01 00
10 9 8 7 6 5 4 3 2 1

**Library of Congress Cataloging-in-Publication Data**
Schaefer, Lola M.,
    Supermarket / by Lola M. Schaefer.
      p. cm. – (Who works here?)
    Includes bibliographical references and index.
    Summary: An introduction to the people who work in a supermarket, including the
store manager, bakery manager, butcher, grocery clerk, cashier, and others.
    ISBN 1-57572-518-5 (lib. bdg.)
    1. Supermarkets—Juvenile literature. [1. Supermarkets. 2. Occupations.] I. Title. II.
Series.
    HF5469.S29 2000
    381'.148—dc21                                         99-040769
                                                          CIP

**Acknowledgments**
All photographs by Phil Martin.

Special thanks to Rick Wicknick and all the workers at Eagle Country Maket in Elgin, Illinois,
and to workers everywhere who take pride in what they do.

Every effort has been made to contact copyright holders of any material reproduced in this book.
Any omissions will be rectified in subsequent printings if notice is given to the publisher.

Some words are shown in bold, **like this.**
You can find out what they mean by looking in the glossary.

# Contents

# What Is a Supermarket?

A supermarket is a **business** that sells fresh food and groceries. Store workers put the groceries on display so **customers** can come and buy what they need. Most supermarkets are open from early morning until late night.

A supermarket wants to sell the finest food. An important job is keeping all food fresh and safe to eat. Many people work together in a supermarket. They want their store to be a friendly place for customers to buy good food.

This supermarket is in Elgin, Illinois. The map shows all of the places where the people in this book are working. Many supermarkets in the United States look like this.

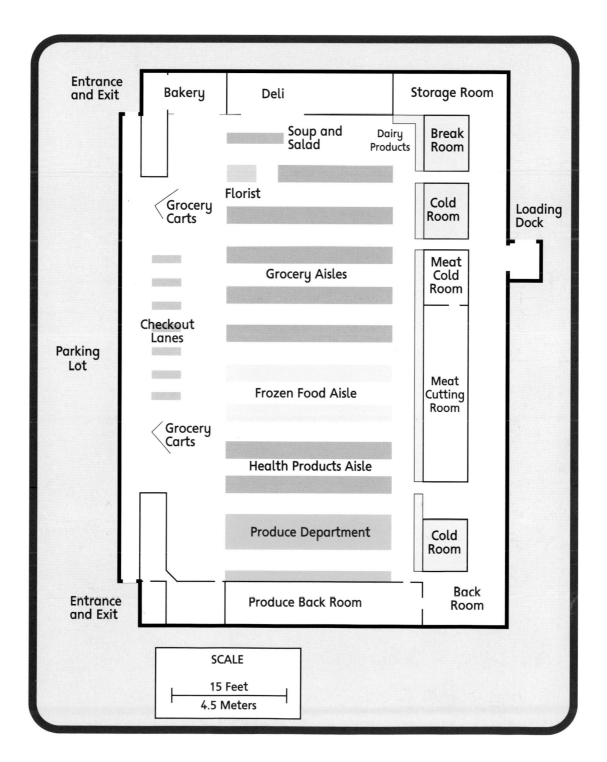

Entrance and Exit

Bakery

Deli

Storage Room

Soup and Salad

Dairy Products

Break Room

Florist

Grocery Carts

Cold Room

Loading Dock

Meat Cold Room

Grocery Aisles

Checkout Lanes

Parking Lot

Meat Cutting Room

Frozen Food Aisle

Grocery Carts

Health Products Aisle

Produce Department

Cold Room

Entrance and Exit

Produce Back Room

Back Room

SCALE

15 Feet

4.5 Meters

# Store Manager

Most supermarkets have a store manager. The store manager is in charge of everything that happens in the supermarket. The store manager hires all the people who work in the store. He or she explains the rules to the **employees** and shows them how to do their jobs.

The store manager at this supermarket is Rich. Rich often talks with employees before the store opens.

Many store managers work ten years or more in a supermarket before becoming a store manager. They learn how to do many different jobs, which helps them know the needs of the employees. The store manager sets a good example by being cheerful and hardworking.

Here, Rich and the **deli** manager plan the needs of the deli department.

# Office Manager

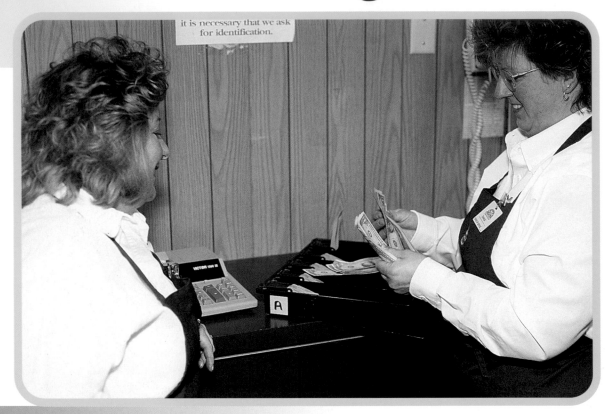

Kathleen (on the left) is the office manager at this supermarket. Here, she watches a cashier count the money in the drawer.

An office manager prepares the **cash drawers** for the cashiers. Every morning he or she puts money in the cash drawers. During the day, the office manager cashes checks for **customers**. Later in the day, the office manager checks the money in the cash drawers with the sales at each **cash register**.

Office managers keep **records** of all sales in the supermarket. They need to have good math skills and work carefully so they don't make mistakes. Because office managers handle all the money in the supermarket, they need to be honest people.

Kathleen also helps customers all day.

# Deli Manager

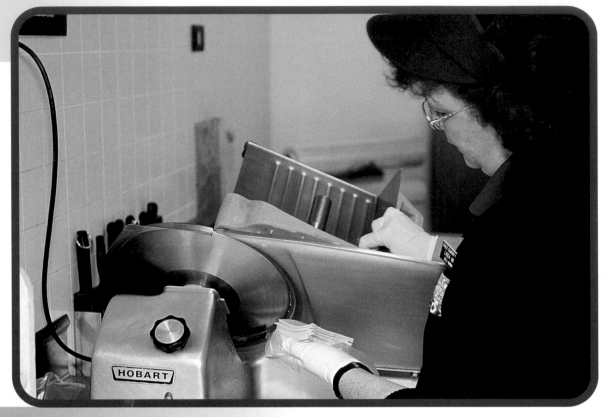

The deli manager at this supermarket is
Linda. Slicers are sharp and cut easily,
so Linda is careful when slicing foods.

The **deli** manager is in charge of preparing and
selling the food in the deli department. Linda
and the other deli workers make sandwiches and
fry chicken in the morning. Then, they make the
soup and salads for the day. Later, they slice
meats and cheeses for the **customers**.

Most deli managers were deli workers before they became managers. Deli managers make sure the hot food is cooked properly. They check the ovens and warmers every morning to make sure they are working correctly. Meat must be cooked well to kill all **bacteria.**

Deli workers fill the soup and salad bar each morning for the customers.

# Bakery Manager

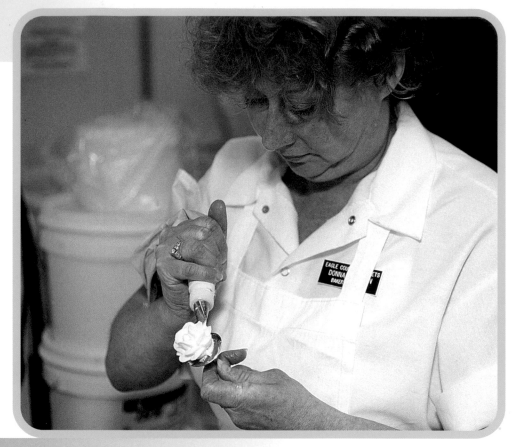

Donna, a bakery manager at the supermarket, makes a rose with frosting for a cake.

The bakery manager is a person who is in charge of all the food made and sold in the bakery. Early in the morning, she or he fries doughnuts and bakes breads. Later in the day, the bakery manager bakes cookies, cakes, and brownies. Bakers enjoy decorating the baked goods to please the **customers**.

Donna, like many bakery managers, learned her job by working in the bakery for a few years. A bakery manager orders all the mixes for baked goods. He or she trains new **employees** in the bakery. The manager and other bakers always wear white aprons and hair nets while working in the bakery.

The bakery is filled with baked goods for customers by 7:00 A.M.

# Meat Manager

Jim is a meat manager and butcher at this supermarket. He and the butchers in the meat department wear long white coats to protect their clothes.

Meat managers are responsible for all the meat sold to **customers**. They and the other **butchers** cut big pieces of meat with a saw. They cut and trim smaller pieces of meat with a knife. All the meat is prepared in a cold room that is 50°Fahrenheit (10° Celsius).

It takes most meat managers three years to learn how to prepare and package meat. During this time, they learn how to keep the cold room and tools free of **bacteria**. Every day, the butchers **disinfect** the machines and countertops with soap and water. This helps keep the meat safe to eat.

Here, Jim places meat into a display case.

# Using a Meat Packaging Machine and Grinder

Cheira enters a code into the machine. This code tells the computer what price and date to print on the meat packages.

The meat manager and his staff use a meat packaging machine to save time and work. The meat wrapper **programs** the computer in the machine with the different cuts and kinds of meat. Then, the machine wraps the tray of meat in plastic and stamps the weight and price on it.

The meat manager uses a meat grinder to make hamburger and other ground meats. They place the extra meat from steaks and roasts into the bin at the top. Blades inside the meat grinder crush the meat. The meat manager wants the meat ground three times before it is sold to the **customer**.

Jim puts fresh beef into the meat grinder.

# Produce Manager

Richard is the produce manager. Here,
he makes a display of oranges.

A produce manager is in charge of the food and workers
in the produce department. He or she orders all the fruit
and vegetables for the store. Produce workers display the
fruit by mixing the colors on the table. Everyday they take
the unfresh vegetables from the rack and add fresh ones.

A produce manager trains for the job by being a produce worker for a few years. One of the responsibilities of a produce manager is that he or she meets with **state health inspectors** when they visit the supermarket. Together, they check that the misting system, produce cooler, and drains are clean and working well.

A produce worker freshens the greens on the vegetable rack.

# Automatic Misting System

Cool water sprays over the vegetables in a fine mist.

Produce managers rely on the misting system to help
keep vegetables fresh. A misting system hangs above
the vegetable rack. Every eighteen minutes, the small
**nozzles** spray water over the vegetables. The mist lasts
for eighteen seconds. Vegetables need cool air and
moisture to stay fresh.

Produce managers store extra fruit and vegetables in the produce cooler. The cooler is a large, **refrigerated** room in the back of the supermarket. If fresh food freezes, it spoils. So, the temperature in the cooler is kept above freezing. It is set between 38° and 42° Fahrenheit (3° to 5° Celsius).

A produce worker takes carrots from the cooler to be put on display for the **customers.**

# Grocery Clerk

Rob is a grocery clerk at this supermarket. Here, he fills a display.

The first job of a grocery clerk is to keep the shelves in the store full of food for the **customers.** He or she also unloads the trucks, stacks the food in the back room, and builds displays throughout the store. Whenever customers cannot find items, a grocery clerk can help them.

Grocery clerks use many tools. One of these is the order gun. When the store sells a lot of one item, the grocery clerk scans that item to order more. The laser in the gun reads the bar code and sends a message to the main computer in the store. The computer puts the item on an order form.

Rob orders more soap quickly and easily with the order gun.

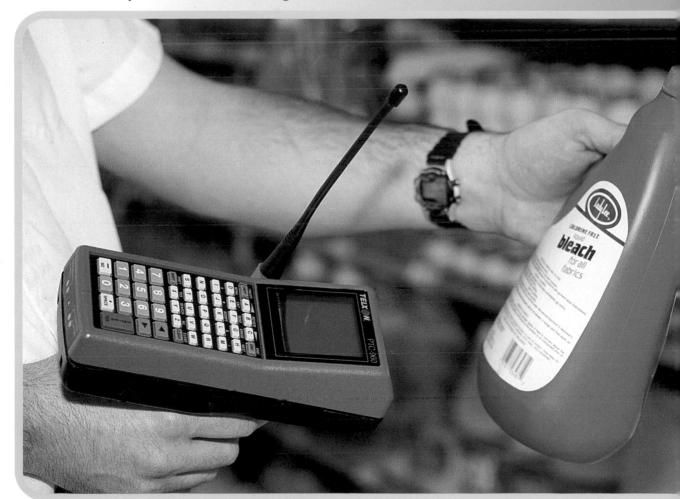

# Cashier

Sharon is a cashier. She scans a box
of tissues to **record** the price.

A cashier greets **customers** as they come into
the checkout lane. She or he pulls the customer's
food across the scanner, subtracts the coupons, and
asks for payment. Many times the cashier helps the
utility clerk put the groceries into bags.

Cashiers train with other cashiers to learn the job. They learn how to work the **cash register.** They learn the different codes for fresh fruit and vegetables. Cashiers carefully watch for torn packages and then replace them for the customer.

Sharon counts the correct change as she puts it in the customer's hand.

# Using Bar Codes and Laser Scanners

PROOF OF PURCHASE

0  15100 00031  7

All food sold in a supermarket has a bar code on the outside of the package.

Bar codes help the cashier record the correct cost of a grocery item. A bar code is a pattern of black bars and white spaces. Each pattern is different. The code stands for letters and numbers. A laser scanner can read a bar code forward or backward.

Cashiers cannot read bar codes, but a laser scanner can. The white spaces between the black lines reflect the laser rays. This sends a coded message to the computer in the **cash register.** Then, the item and price are printed on the cash register tape.

Here, laser rays scan a box at the checkout lane.

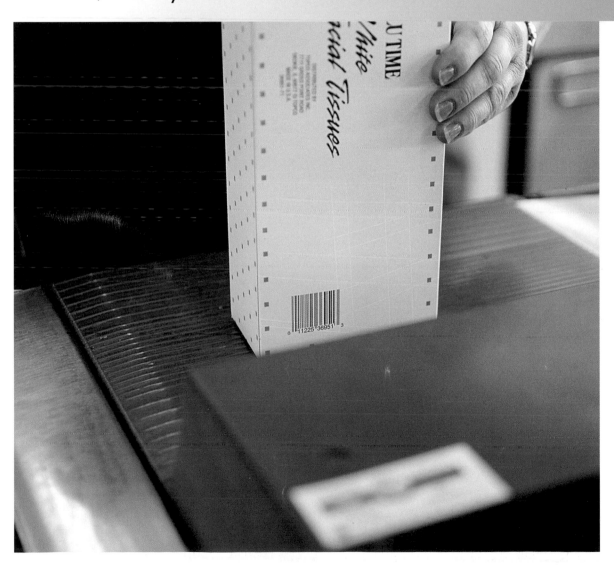

# Utility Clerk

Fred is a utility clerk at the supermarket. Part of his job is to put groceries into a customer's cart.

Utility clerks bag groceries. Before they begin, they ask **customers** if they would like plastic or paper bags. They always put soaps and cold products in separate bags. Utility clerks try to help customers as they leave the store.

During their supermarket training, utility clerks learn how to help out in other parts of the store. They bring the grocery carts from the parking lot into the store. They put the returned plastic bags into a **recycle** bin. Utility clerks mop up spills and keep the store floor clean of all trash.

Fred loads groceries into this customer's car.

# Glossary

**bacteria** microscopic living things; some are useful in the human body, but others can cause disease

**business** company that makes, buys, or sell things

**butcher** someone who cuts meat into pieces for people to buy and cook

**cash drawer** drawer of money in the cash register

**cash register** business machine that records sales on a receipt. All cash registers have a display for the total sales and a cash drawer.

**customer** person who shops and buys in a store

**deli** (short for delicatessen) place where prepared foods, such as salads and cooked meats, are sold

**disinfect** to make something free of germs

**employee** person who works for someone else and is paid to do so

**nozzle** spout that sprays liquid from a tube or hose

**program** to put instructions or information into a computer

**records** information written in an orderly manner

**recycle** to process old paper, plastic, or glass so it can be used in new products

**refrigerated** kept cool or cold

**state health inspectors** people hired by the state government to make sure all businesses and their products are safe for the public

# More Books to Read

Bendick, Jeanne, and Robert Bendick. *Markets: From Barter to Bar Codes.* New York: Franklin Watts, 1997.

Flanagan, Alice K. *A Busy Day at Mr. Kang's Grocery Store.* New York: Children's Press, 1996.

Gisler, Maria. *Food.* Lincolnwood, Ill.: VGM Career Horizons, 1997.

Hautzig, David. *At the Supermarket.* New York: Orchard Books, 1994.

Wheeler, Jill C. *The Food We Eat.* Edina, Minn.: ABDO and Daughters, 1991.

# Index